I0755984

FINISHING LINE PRESS
www.finishinglinepress.com

WHAT FLOWERS MAY COME

poems by

Sarah Durrand

Finishing Line Press
Georgetown, Kentucky

WHAT FLOWERS MAY COME

ISBN 979-8-89990-366-3 First Edition

ACKNOWLEDGMENTS

"Wild grass," "THE MOON," "Blue pansies," "Sunflower dreams," "In the backyard," and "At Monet's water lilies" were previously published online by *inparentheses.art*
"Desert verbena" and "Citrus pleasure, pt. ii" were previously published online as part of *bloodtreeliterature.com*
"Red Admiral" was previously published online by *blackhorsereview.com*
"Raindrops after rain" was previously published online by *halfandone.com*
"In betrayal of Pablo Neruda" was first published in *Orca, A Literary Journal,* (orcalit.com)
"Montana bluegrass" was previously published online as part of *theclosedeyeopen.com* and *cathexisnorthwestpress.com*

Thank you to my parents, Cheryl and Chris, for telling me to write; to my friends who read what I write; and to the people, animals, and plants who give me beautiful things to write about. Thank you deeply to my husband, Colin, for supporting me through every step. I love it all, but I love you most of all.

Publisher: Leah Huete de Maines
Editor: Christen Kincaid
Cover Art: Sarah Durrand
Author Photo: Sarah Durrand
Cover Design: Elizabeth Maines McCleavy

Order online: www.finishinglinepress.com
also available on amazon.com

Author inquiries and mail orders:
Finishing Line Press
PO Box 1626
Georgetown, Kentucky 40324
USA

Contents

WILD GRASS

We were told as children
that each blade of grass
has millions of microscopic
hooks
and that's why it feels
itchy on our legs and backs
and almost sticky on our
fingers.

I should like to lay you
in a field of tall,
wild grass,
breathing in the breeze,
hook myself to you
stuck together some
distance from the
train tracks—

scratch this itch
and see if it lingers.

A PERSIMMON FOR YOU, FOR ME

A persimmon to deliver, to carry my heavy
soul through a train ride, the promise of riots.
A candle from a year ago burning -
what does the long-settled,
now-singed dust add? And
just how bad is paraffin wax?

A year ago—it was different, I
was less concerned with
plant-based tealights and
the nostalgia of honeycomb
cereal. Now, on the precipice of
an unknown reckoning, I learn:
all moments are inevitable;
their meanings are not.

Is thirty aged enough to buy
vintage kitchenware? I miss
the already-old feeling of a
lemon rind, throbbing against
the juicer in my palm. I miss
the wire cheese slicer, lost
somewhere on a mountain
I no longer visit. Sure, metal
can be lead, and glass
can shatter. But a headline
warns me: throw away
your black utensils. So is an
irradiated plate much worse?

I dream the radio doesn't work, I
dream the front door charm is
missing. I dream my brother is
trapped underground. I dream I do
decide to buy honeycomb cereal.
I wake up exhausted by
all the places my soul is touched,
reusable bags under my eyes.

A simple persimmon will take me
through to this time next week:
I'll be home, I'll know more.
I'll burn sage for the second time,
think about my vices, maybe
cry, maybe pray, and decide
what I pray to. For now,
I create space in the backyard
to drink strong green tea and
enjoy the feeling of finishing
things, not things finishing.
To watch hummingbirds and
wait desperately for chimes to sound,
to think there's local beekeepers
around me who might share
their wax. To take care to smile
at the waving trees, to remember
how simply I'd write about golden hills.

To wonder what comes next for
the crows I yesterday gave my bread to,
like a suiciding witch losing her belongings.

To wait for what comes next,
for you and for me.

DOWN HERE

This small town is about
midnight bike rides
and midday storms,
the biggest questions,
corn fields somewhere I've never seen,
small triumphs I've never dreamed
and just a few more stars in the dark.

We read, we write,
we drop our pens and paper
to walk the middle of fields
to gaze at the sky,
to wonder
what the *hell* and *why*
we're to do
down here.

IN BETRAYAL OF PABLO NERUDA

I read Pablo Neruda awestruck,
jaw dropped and glass shattered
at the bloody hibiscus thrusting,
the pulsing violent staking of claims.

I stare at you with a lead heart,
soul sobbing and stomach nauseated
that words fail in the barrel
of my smoking gun mouth.
I sputter and choke on bullets,
painstakingly mutter, "you are like a mountain" -

In betrayal of the poet.
For you're a black hole,
central and impossibly deep,
pulling me thoughtlessly, throbbing,
confident that the stars and suns
and my world will collapse for you,
my limbs flail, submissive to your keep.

If ever there were peace,
it was a quiet, soft, clear afternoon
on the shore of a teal lake.
But you ruin it when you tell me
I'm building a fairy home.
I bite my tongue and swallow my secrets.
I don't tell you I build delicate things
because I'm stuck in a dreamstate,
a lethal spider's silk,
in stagnation, afraid to snap—

I almost asphyxiate on the drive home
because, in truth,
I'd vomit bullets,
I'd swan-dive into the sun,
I'd pump a pinecone through my heart,
and I'd crush a hundred fairies
to know you'd make love to me in the dust.

STAMEN

Explore all visions and possibilities thoroughly
is what my mama and tarot card told me—

Vision three:
I don't think they expected I'd have a dream
I was indebted to a demon
with four muscled arms
holding me in place,
that it would be violence,
that I'd find comfort in the chokehold—
Cognizant of cognitive dissonance
in commitment of a forced mission,
but indulgent of another, less.
In identity crisis she asks,
why can't two truths live at once?

Vision two:
The day I thought I'd leave this house for good
I saw an orange-crowned warbler
and two dark-eyed juncos
flitting in the underbrush out back—
In simpler terms:
not the usual birds
for not the usual times.

Vision one:
Days before the birds, the dream, the demon,
you bought me flowers and four hadn't bloomed yet.
"I'm looking forward to them opening;
they looked so cool at the shop—"
So do I focus on their arrival,
beautiful and fragrant, though delayed,
or that you once again brokered me a promise?
You're fascinated by the stamen
with rust-brown pollen finally,
willingly on your fingertips -
But, with all your lip service,
how didn't you know
what a lily was?

YOU GOT AN OFFICE JOB

Rare awareness in the difference of how we both experience time—our bodies almost always within each other, life so spaciously shared; you—interview, early, driving, slow. me—2:47 came quick. Wondering how it's going, how you're feeling, if you're out of breath or cool and collected. Things I normally know by the bumps and breezes of the house when you're wandering around it and I'm at my desk downstairs. I have known your every moment for years, we've shared every minute and speck of dust. It's strange to know you're away and that you might have dark evening commutes and lunches out and a tucked-away office while I hold down our emptier home, feeding the cats and talking more out loud in your absence. Sadness for the life we've lived so together, that how we carry forward together in time may split. Fear that your day might go hard and slow while mine fast and breezy and I won't know until the garage door quietly lifts. By rusty springs I'll see your face and it's anxiety hoping I still understand your expressions while seeing them less, instead of in all the mornings and corners as usual. I'll miss the small coughs and I'll wonder if the house looks different to you when you come back to me each day.

OREGANO

Taking stock of life I don't typically think of the
three-ninety-nine plastic jar of oregano I
bought when I was twenty-three. I picked herbs
and spices because I had heard of them, not
because I had ever cooked with them or was
thinking of a recipe. That studio apartment with
its cornflower door was a recipe for, a portal to,
a good start to the rest of my life, which would
of course be brimming with oregano.

Seven years and a new apartment later, have I
shaken that jar more than twice? It's stuffed in
a beautiful, messy cabinet with cardamom seeds
and endless cumin; even a "pumpkin spice" and
dill. So many herbs and flavors each with
their own half-life and urgency of repurchase.
Yet this dried oregano in its plastic jar, probably
plastic we don't use anymore, probably leeching,
probably plastic oregano in its plastic glossy
red cap, it just sits and sits and I never, ever
grab it except to rummage for anything else.

I've proudly entered a phase of life in which
I use things, and use them up. "*To enjoy the
feeling of finishing things, not things finishing*"
I write. I grow sage for smudging and nip
for the cats; I grow rosemary and lavender
for the bees and pinch basil and thyme. I
desperately fight to keep mint alive and
occasionally try parsley again, for tea. Peppers
and potatoes find a life and a home with me. But
I've never bought an oregano plant and
I've never made a plan.

Future: Two cities and three houses away, maybe
a couple kids (surely given fresher, better oregano),
the loss of parents and siblings and friends,
regime changes and moves and pregnancy and
grief and this little jar of tiny, mild, mediterranean
chopped dried leaves will see me through it all,
like some ghost of how many whims never make
it to action, and how we all aspire for far too much.

CITRUS PLEASURE, PT. I

I shall live in a house with a lemon tree
and when I'm feeling lemony,
I'll take a fruit from my lemon tree
and sip my freshly lemoned tea.

I shall live in a house with someone I love
and when I'm feeling beaten and shoved,
I'll wrap in the arms of the person I love -
my love and my lemons will rise above.

NUTMEG

Hmmmm
Like the taste of tiki
with bone broth,
you linger falsely in
memories of dimly-lit
caverns (which
weren't playing this
twinkly music,
either.)

But the feeling of nostalgia
in ground nutmeg,
and the vision of you
against flames flickering
in red glass jars,

Well, it's as good as truth to me.

And what matter is truth?
Cream, and iced coffee,
paintings of earth-toned circles,
imagined conversations,
dark rum, and
dream interpretation journals
suspended by ropes
against half-moons…!

Blessed solstice, secret lover.
—synapses fire, overwhelmed.

RAINDROPS AFTER RAIN

It's the end of the year
in the backyard again—
raindrops after rain
have coalesced on the windchimes,
the fence, the hummingbird feeder,
like soft icicles on trees
in crystalline waiting,
like a thousand swords of Damocles.

One lemon fell off the tree this season.
riper than the others by a dozen lemon-years.
Shrouded by leaves and tucked in the back,
it screamed for the next step,
demanded all from its home,
turned too-dark yellow and
thudded into the weeds.

When did it die?
When its stem started loosening,
when the last fiber snapped?
When it bruised on impact,
or when it stopped rolling?
When it started to rot in vain?
When I noticed it and couldn't eat it,
or when I threw it away?
Could it have been as early as
when it started to swell ahead of season?
Could it not bear the winter?
And was that by choice
or its embedded fate?

This morning, the tree is abundant
with lemons that waited.
I pull, some a little underripe,
but that's hardly an issue
when they're used or given away.
Sour is easier to swallow than mold,

sour can be sweetened,
what's dead can only be cut away.

No birds back here right now,
no breeze to disturb what's dangling in wait.
At the risk of those thousand swords,
and with clairvoyance that
one drop could end it all,
I gently push the windchimes.
Funny how even when I'm the wind,
I still don't know how the bells will toll.

GERANIUMS

Give me—burnt coffee, hot
mountains, a goose honk
inland, imagined. Geraniums
in garden defiance, growing
growing growing. Give me
black scattered poppy seeds
and memories of snatched
walnuts, trespassed orchards,
green. Give me him, beard,
fishnets, bored; tell me it
doesn't turn me on. Give
me hot and bothered in a
cold mountain lake, eyeing
two hundred thirty pounds of
you—caffeinated, wet, ready
to take. Give me blueberries
while you tell me we could
never work; give me your
mouth and prove it.

DESERT VERBENA

I like desert washes because
they have one place to go—
they show a clear path,
and I could follow them for hours
until I find the end I'm chasing
(which I'm sure is just around
the next bend,
within the next mile,
beyond those purple flowers,
at that mountain in the distance.)

I'd consider myself lucky
if I came to a desert wash
on the rare, rained day when
it could carry me away.
I'd lay on my back without hesitation,
skin cracking like hardened mud,
gratefully drinking drops from gray clouds.
I wouldn't look where I was going—
close my eyes, flood, savor the flow.

What a blessing to ride the torrent,
to float and thrash above the wash,
because, most days,
I just kick up sand:
dry, rested, purgatory, still.
Movement elusive except my own
towards the promise of one more bend,
some new view of those purple flowers.

BUTTERFLY PEA FLOWER TEA

With more forethought
(and less anxiety)
I could have asked if
you still like purple.
I would have brought you
butterfly pea flower tea
and a homegrown lemon,
told you how a squeeze of citrus
brews a little magic,
could have made you smile
like we were seventeen.

Instead, I'm feverishly dreaming
of breaking sticks to feed to cows,
skinny-dipping on summer days,
what I think your face looked like
when you were surprised,
remembering what gifts you gave me
and wondering where they went.
Picturing all the ways you must have looked
while I was looking somewhere else.

Like a lemon and some loose-leaf tea
could make you think it's different now.
You had so much to give—
I had so much to take.

THE MOON

You read online
after hours of aimless
staring at web pages
that Jupiter is the
closest it's been in
fifty-nine years
and you can even see
a moon on it with
just binoculars.

At 2 a.m. you took
your binoculars
and bravely went to the curb
30 feet from your house.
You saw a speck—
THE MOON
—but it danced and zigged
because your hands aren't steady
and your binoculars are cheap.

You went back inside.

CITRUS PLEASURE, PT. II

Encased in sun, in the middle of meditation,
my mouth waters for lemonade.
A breakthrough, maybe?
I notice myself breathing in
A moment of presence and gratitude
I notice myself breathing out
for squeezed juice stirred with sugar
in a yellow pitcher, with a wooden spoon.
I notice myself breathing in
I've waited so long for this harvest and
am reminded of the power in waiting
I notice myself breathing out
for I've begun to notice how the sounds differ
between backyard birds, and a deeper flap
I notice myself breathing in
catches and pulls my thoughts outward.
Discipline keeps my eyes closed
I notice myself breathing out
—my thoughts, less so.

A chime marks the end of my session
and scares the mystery bird away before
I can say hello. Six pulled lemons sit in two rows.

The air smells like smoke today.
And I thought the tree trimming would
drive the birds away
but the sun is strong and
a couple more moments means
a yellow bird comes back,
with a black throat and a deep flap,
eventually the smoke dissipates,
and more lemons ripen for the drinking.

Maybe, like how fruit grows
more abundantly when pruned,
the birds appreciate tidying, too.

WETLANDS

There are places
where the water melds
with the land,
flesh with each other,
shimmering and wet
and soft and lush—

The river seeps from the ground,
the sky lays the ground flat with the river.
Life is created and unthinkingly expands.

Here, the earth is teeming and whole.

I'm not sure if you're water or earth,
but outside your covers seems barren and cold.

BLUE PANSIES

I got home and
frantically flipped through
seed catalogs,
desperate to find
you in nature.

Your eyes are far beyond
blue pansies,
but they were the
closest I came.

DAISIES

Kiss me atop a golden hill
with lips hot as coffee
and delicate as
early-june daisies.

Meet me under the
tallest oak tree
and caffeinate me
like crazy.

MONTANA BLUEGRASS

Dream of me like Montana bluegrass,
subtle and attuned to the
breeze around me.

I'll dream of you like a
westbound train pouring over its tracks,
loud and complex and beautiful and
gone.

I'll bend a little deeper with the wind in your wake.

POPPIES

Parsley, sage, rosemary and
time, saliva, desire. There's
abundance in watching him drag
a wagon with plants overflowing,
something succulent in the air.
Like a bird drawn to seed, I glance
him standing by the gate, debate
buying soil so he'll carry it, to dirty
his hands, his shirt, his neck,
his mind, all spotted and
sweat as he toils after me.

I don't ask for help, show
him I don't need it, keep
my own secret garden, to not
cross that line. Makes it all
the more sweet and honeydew
to catch him watch me walk away.
We smile, peripheral. I know where
to find him and only I decide when,
but his sunglasses hide gaze—I'm
at his mercy, on full display,
with wildly picked Iceland
poppies in my hands.

IN THE BACKYARD

Red wine and succulents,
impish thoughts, petulant,
a hot and wistful temperament—
my mind falls skyward
to you.

Gently swaying pink hibiscus;
I'm not saying that I miss this
but image: you, barely dressed—
my heart falls wayward
to you.

Mint and basil blooming west,
begging of us spooning best;
tonight and then: ruined rest—
as I collapse inward
on you.

DAHLIA

At the county fair,
always hot dusty summer
golden hay-aired day
I walk into a room of dahlias.

and sure, roses, but the dahlias
Catch my eye,
the biggest, you, right there:
white, cupping petals,
red splatters,
diamond patterned
crystal vase, clear water,
stand tall.

An annual trip
to my annual wondering
about the people that plant these,
about your secret life
when I'm not looking at you.

What leaves did you wear in the garden?
Where else do you bloom but for me?

SUNFLOWER DREAMS

He probably has an actual bed
(which is something anyone else would assume)—
but my visions take place on a mattress
overflowing a frame,
low to the ground,
where the quiet sounds of us
pour onto the floor and
spill outward the walls,
lapping against dark, dirty hardwood.
Sunlight splashes through a window
through which we could see
Presidio Park—

like the light is yellow petals
and, in our hideaway,
we're the interwoven seeds.

AT MONET'S WATER LILIES

You looked lovely
standing in front of
the impressionists.

You're so self-assured
yet the negative space
in a dreamy pond
commands you.

Now, instead of
driving
and heat,
you talk of
bridges at dawn,

and instead of
"behold the man,"
you want a tattoo
of a water lily.

Pastels and softness
are a strange relief
upon you.

RED ADMIRAL

Lemons, lemons, lemons, LEMONS,
Was it this time last year I was replete with lemons?
Because as time marches on, so produces this tree,
and it only occurred to me tonight,
after three years of tending,
that maybe I'm reaping the work I sew.

It never feels earned, to me;
it feels happenstance,
more like a reward not for
being or doing so,
but for listening,
intuitively,
carefully.

Luck requires sacredness
(which requires a nicer word, *sacracy*).
I've learned you must ask a butterfly to beat the clouds away
and nod to the crows when you see them,
watch the swallows dive from not any patch of grass,
but the exact one small flowers coaxed you to—
understand they love the sun more than you ever will,
ask about cardinals the second you think to,
lay wildflowers on bloated rodents.
And finally, have faith to take off your glasses
and look into the eclipse,
that great black hole in the sky.

*

It's rare to know you're exactly where you should be.
Bring lemonade everywhere you go
and give away all you can.
Tell your family it will be okay,
but don't tell them how you know.
Your life always changes in three minutes or less.

PRICKLY PEAR

Oh, the parrots have a lot to squawk about in heat like this.

We on the ground, in the shade of porches,
are silent as we look to the trees,
ever more aware in battery fires and
ninety-three degree mornings
just how flammable they are.
We remember the ash, and the
video camera crackling branches
as horses were freed from the ranch.

Fall is the harvest, the gratitude.
I'm grateful for window unit ACs and
for the baby succulents out back,
that the hidden snake didn't bite me
as I inquired after prickly pear.
I left the fruit for the canyon critters,
as the rattler left its poison for me.

I worry I don't honor my elders enough,
my garden enough, my lovers enough.
I write letters to young voters while
praying I'm not missing the smoke alarm,
drowned out by the blast of that privileged,
conditioned, safe and loud air.
I hate sleeping with it on.
Shuttered from the world and
deaf to nighttime whispers -
If there's a siren, I'd like to know.

So why I eagerly went out to sweat
and look for green feathers in the trees.
But found I was only hearing echoes—
dry wind was fluttering the leaves,
loud squawks dissipated,
flown off toward the coast.

And there's me: standing with
unfocused binoculars in the wrong direction,
grateful for lenses to help me see the fire coming,
at the cost of watching the rest fly away.

DIABETIC COLORACIDOSIS

I've learned a lot about colors lately. Like
who knew the halfway point between a
wishing-for-autumn persimmon and a
relishing-the-spring lavender is a soft and
neon peach, like the wink and nod of
saying *stonefruit* when you're older (but
young enough to die good), like the tree in
your favorite park you've never stolen fruit from—

and may have never have. Because
who knew my guardian angel was gray,
wings wrapping me in the back of
an ambulance? Who knew a hospital
room could warmly hum beige in a long
afternoon waiting to go home? Who knew
mossy teal scrubs would comfort me
and verdantly green backyard trees
would make me cry, happy to be
home and alive to buy rose-pink ink
and burn my thumb with matches?

I pick carefully the color of heart I
send to friends in texts; I deliberate
thoroughly the merit of every sunset.

GALAXIAL

Contrary to researchers' tired deliberations,
I write to assure you that dreams are,
with certainty, for psychic cleansing.
That's why I can only write them
on overcast mornings, when a dewy
cloud layer keeps those sleepy images
trapped in the air, long enough
to pull from above clairvoyant,
shimmering threads of meaning
(an act that is absolutely assumptive
and absurd, and also, sometimes,
absolute)—

Anyway,
          it was about you, of course,
and it was about me.
It was about speaking without fear
and I think it was a closing.
          Because it sure looked like *Riverworld*
from that dusty book on the cabin shelf,
and, naturally, we walked in a verdant park
under a pink purple green speckled universe.

And then it was your apartment,
          and then it was your arms.
Too messy, too thin, I gleaned it as
the iridescent wing of some
          distant butterfly's flap, I
I felt the ego death of curiosity:
unafraid to share my feelings;
          at peace they couldn't last.

It's always a sign when dream time
          aligns with real time.
I knew dawn would bring the end,
and we talked, and you said nice things,

but I was ready to bid you farewell—
another life, another time.
I wondered my way to a breakthrough and
learned I'm allowed to be a mystery myself.

As the sun rose between your arms I prayed,
Reverence to honesty as indulgence;
reverence to stars in the sky.

Sarah Durrand is a solar-powered poet, novice gardener, and lover of all small critters. A lifelong hobby writer, her parents told her "whatever you do in life, you need to write", which gave her the appropriate jolt to start getting her work published (thanks, Mom and Dad!) When not writing, she enjoys reading, rollerblading, and talking about the birds that visit her bird feeder. She lives in San Diego with her husband and two very chatty cats, all of whom are lovingly tolerant of her ever-changing projects and crafts. *WHAT FLOWERS MAY COME* is Sarah's first published chapbook; she is additionally grateful to have had her poetry included in prior publications listed on her website at *www.sarahdurrand.com.*

www.ingramcontent.com/pod-product-compliance
Lightning Source LLC
LaVergne TN
LVHW090540110826
845146LV00003B/1200

* 9 7 9 8 8 9 9 9 0 3 6 6 3 *